Pocket guide

Your Rights at Work

LAWPACK

Pocket guide

Your Rights at Work

by Melanie Slocombe

The author

Melanie Slocombe is a partner in the London office of the
international law firm McDermott Will & Emery, where she
specialises in employment law.

Your Rights at Work
by Melanie Slocombe

Lawpack Publishing Limited
76–89 Alscot Road
London SE1 3AW

www.lawpack.co.uk

ISBN: 1 904053 83 1

The law is stated as at 1 April 2005

Valid in England & Wales and Scotland

Exclusion of Liability and Disclaimer

While every effort has been made to ensure that this Lawpack Pocket Guide
provides accurate and expert guidance, it is impossible to predict all the
circumstances in which it may be used. Accordingly, neither the publisher,
author, retailer nor any other suppliers shall be liable to any person or entity
with respect to any loss or damage caused or alleged to be caused by the
information contained in or omitted from this Lawpack Pocket Guide.

For convenience (and for no other reason), 'him', 'he' and 'his' have been used
throughout and should be read to include 'her', 'she' and 'her'.

Contents

Introduction

Few legal fields change as rapidly as employment law. New laws, economic policy changes, trade union practices and the tremendous impact of membership of the European Union all mean that employment law is constantly being tested, reshaped and redefined.

The idea of taking legal action against your employer has become increasingly acceptable in recent years. Many of the recent employment laws are intended to replace the notion of conflict between employers and employees with the promotion of partnership and the encouragement of flexible working. The practical effect of these new laws is to increase your rights in the workplace and to place an even greater responsibility on your employer to ensure that it complies with its new 'employee friendly' obligations. It is therefore very important that you know how you are protected in the workplace.

One of the purposes of this book is to promote good communications in the workplace. It may draw your attention to areas of potential or actual conflict. When they arise, disputes can usually be resolved through deliberate, honest negotiation. No employer enjoys having to take disciplinary action – let alone dismiss an employee – because of the sense of failure it frequently brings on both sides. But if your employer considers that dismissal is the only course of action, it still must carry it out in a legally acceptable way.

This Guide provides a broad overview of your rights and duties as an employee. It will alert you to the conditions, practices, responsibilities, duties and remedies that fall within the scope of employment law, and help you navigate your way through them.

CHAPTER 1

Applying for a job

Even before you start a new job, you are protected by the law. This chapter gives you a summary of your rights when you apply for work, starting with the law on discrimination.

Discrimination

No matter whether recruitment is carried out through employment agencies, job centres, careers offices or schools, prospective employers have a duty not to discriminate. They must neither give instructions nor bring pressure to discriminate.

It is unlawful for employers to advertise vacancies, select interview candidates or offer employment in a way that discriminates on the following grounds:

- **Sex**
- **Race**
- **Marital status**
- **Gender reassignment (i.e. sex change)**
- **Sexual orientation**
- **Religion/religious belief**
- **Disability**

If you are applying for a job and you feel that you have been discriminated against on any of these grounds, you can raise a complaint with the Equal Opportunities Commission, the Disability Rights Commission or an employment tribunal. For more details, see chapter 4 and the 'Useful contacts' section.

There are some jobs for which your sex, race, sexual orientation or religion/religious belief may be a 'genuine occupational qualification'. For example, a Thai restaurant may well want all the waiting staff to be Thai, for authenticity. In these circumstances, discrimination in advertisements, in the interview procedure, in job offers, in offers of promotion, training or transfers is acceptable.

There is currently no express law protecting you from discrimination on the ground of your age, but there is a voluntary code of practice that aims to tackle this problem. The Government has announced proposals to introduce laws to stop age discrimination, which are due to be brought in by December 2006. Also, see chapter 4 on age discrimination as 'unlawful indirect sex discrimination'.

It is unlawful for an employer to refuse employment on the grounds of membership or non-membership of a trade union.

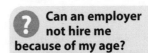

? Can an employer not hire me because of my age?

Yes, for the time being they can, but law changes are planned.

In relation to pregnancy, any decision not to appoint a woman on the ground that she is pregnant is likely to be found to be discriminatory on the ground of her sex.

Employees' criminal convictions

Job applicants can be asked to disclose any criminal convictions and these can be checked with the Criminal Records Bureau, listed under the 'Useful contacts' section at the end of this Guide.

After a certain period of time, people who have been convicted of criminal offences and who have served their sentences are not under a duty to disclose those convictions to a prospective employer. These convictions are known as 'spent' convictions. If spent convictions are disclosed to prospective employers, it is unlawful for them to take the offences into account when considering someone for a job and if they do so, they will be guilty of unlawful discrimination. The periods of time (known as 'rehabilitation periods') depend on the seriousness of the offence; they are set out below. In certain professions, offices and occupations, all previous offences must be disclosed regardless of the period of time that has expired.

Sentence	Rehabilitation period
Imprisonment, corrective training or sentence of detention in a young offenders' institution for between 6 and 30 months	10 years
Imprisonment or sentence of detention in a young offenders' institution for a term not exceeding six months	7 years
A fine or the sentence not expressly covered by the Rehabilitation of Offenders Act 1974	5 years
Order for detention in a detention centre	3 years
Absolute discharge	6 months
Conditional discharge	1 year
Probation	5 years

NB For young offenders, periods are usually reduced by half, except in cases of probation.

Children and 'young persons'

A 'child' is defined as anyone younger than the minimum school-leaving age of 16. A 'young person' is defined as anyone over school-leaving age, but under 18. Young persons are protected by the Working Time Regulations which limit the number of hours young workers may work and provide rules on the daily and weekly rest periods an employer must give to young workers.

No child may be employed:

- if under the age of 13;

- during school hours;

- before 7am or after 7pm;

- for more than two hours on any day when required to attend school;

- for more than two hours on a Sunday;

- in any industrial undertaking; or

- if likely to suffer injury from lifting, carrying or moving heavy items.

> **? Can my son who is 11 get a job as a paperboy?**
>
> *No, children under 13 cannot be employed.*

A local education authority has powers to supervise the employment of school children in its area and may require particulars about a child's employment. It may prohibit or restrict employment if it feels that the employment is unsuitable, even if not unlawful. A person who wishes to employ a child must obtain a permit from the local education authority.

In addition, the Health and Safety Executive (HSE) provides guidance on the employment of younger workers.

Restrictions on employing women

The following restrictions on the employment of women are for the protection of women and it is acceptable to discriminate in employment to comply with these requirements:

- employment in factories within four weeks of childbirth;

- employment in a range of processes involving lead or lead compounds;

- employment in a range of processes in the pottery industry;

- protection from exposure to ionising radiation; and

- employment on ships or aeroplanes while pregnant.

EU and EEA nationals

The member states of the European Union (EU) are: Austria, Belgium, Cyprus, the Czech Republic, Denmark, Estonia, Finland, France, Germany, Greece, Hungary, Ireland, Italy, Latvia, Lithuania, Luxembourg, Malta, the Netherlands, Poland, Portugal, Slovakia, Slovenia, Spain, Sweden and the United Kingdom. The European Economic Area (EEA) comprises EU members plus Iceland, Liechtenstein and Norway.

Citizens of the EU and EEA are known as European Nationals and they do not need work permits; they have the right to come to the UK and look for work. Family members of European Nationals also have an automatic right to accompany such European Nationals to the UK. However, if they wish to stay in the UK for more than six months, they are advised to apply for a residence permit.

Exception

Member states of the EU may reserve certain types of employment in 'public service' for their own nationals, although in practice it has rarely happened; this is an exception to the general rule of free movement of labour within the EU.

Non-EU nationals

If you are not an EU or EEA national, you are subject to immigration control and must obtain a work permit before taking up employment in the UK, unless you belong to one of the categories of people for which this is not necessary.

These include:

- ministers of religion;
- representatives of overseas newspapers, news agencies and broadcasting organisations;
- private servants of diplomatic staff;
- sole representatives of overseas firms;
- teachers and language assistants under approved exchange schemes;
- employees of an overseas government or international organisation;
- seamen under contract to join a ship in British waters;
- operational ground staff of overseas-owned airlines;
- seasonal workers at agricultural camps under approved schemes;
- doctors and dentists in postgraduate training;
- business visitors admitted by the Home Office;
- Commonwealth citizens with the right of abode and those with at least one grandparent born in the UK.

For further details about applications for work permits, contact the Home Office's Work Permits UK Helpline, listed in the 'Useful contacts' section at the end of this Guide.

CHAPTER 2

The employment relationship

Once you have accepted a job offer, the legal relationship with your new employer is governed by two things:

- your 'statutory rights' (i.e. those laid down by law); and

- your contract of employment.

The contract may be verbal or in writing or a mixture of the two and is governed by 'express' terms (written) and 'implied' terms (unwritten, implicit terms such as the duty of good faith) which set out the rights and obligations of you and your employer.

? Does my contract have to cover all my rights?

No, some rights are not included because they are 'statutory' and therefore automatic.

You and your employer are free to agree upon any terms you wish, subject to the statutory rights that are summarised below.

Statutory rights of employees

You automatically become entitled to statutory rights upon entering into an employment contract, without any need for the details of these rights to be written into a contract. A number of these rights depend upon you having a minimum period of employment. The main rights are:

Access to Stakeholder Pensions

If you have at least three months' service working in an organisation with more than five full-time employees, you are entitled to be offered access to a Stakeholder Pension plan by your employer. You do not have to join the plan and your employer does not have to pay any contribution to the plan.

Equal opportunities

See chapter 4.

Equal pay for work of equal value

See chapter 4.

'Guarantee pay'

If you have at least one month's service, you must be paid 'guarantee' payments when you could normally expect to work, but no work is available; the rate is currently £18.40 per day for up to five days in any period of three months. Therefore, the annual maximum is currently £368.

You can complain to an employment tribunal if your employer fails to pay the whole or part of a guarantee payment to which you are entitled; the tribunal can award compensation equal to the amount of the guarantee payment which it finds due.

Healthy and safe working environment

Point of Law
Section 2 Health and Safety at Work etc Act 1974

All employees are entitled to be provided by their employer 'so far as is reasonably practicable' with a safe place to work and safe access to the place of work, a safe system of work, adequate materials, competent fellow employees and protection from unnecessary risk of injury. The Health and Safety Executive (HSE) publishes guidance notes on this subject that are available from HSE Books, listed in the 'Useful contacts' section.

Itemised pay statements

Itemised pay statements must be issued to all employees each time they are paid and these must include the following particulars:

- gross earnings;
- net pay;
- deductions from gross earnings;
- if the net pay is paid in different ways, the amount and method of payment of each part of the payment.

You can complain to an employment tribunal if your employer fails to issue a pay statement or if the content is in dispute.

Maternity rights and benefits

See chapter 3.

National minimum wage (NMW)

You must not be paid less than the NMW. The current rates for the NMW (before deductions for tax and National Insurance contributions) are:

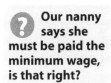 **Our nanny says she must be paid the minimum wage, is that right?**

No, if she works and lives as part of your family, she has no right to it.

- £4.85 per hour for those aged 22 and above (increasing to £5.05 on 1 October 2005, and to £5.35 on 1 October 2006);

- £4.10 per hour for those aged from 18 to 21 and for employees in the first six months of a new job with a new employer who are in specific training (increasing to £4.25 on 1 October 2005, and to £4.45 on 1 October 2006).

Workers aged 16–17 qualify for a third rate of £3 per hour, but apprentices in this age group are exempt.

Employees working and living as part of a family currently have no right to the NMW.

If you do not receive the NMW, you can complain to an employment tribunal. For more details, contact the NMW Helpline on 0845 600 0678 or its website at www.tiger.gov.uk.

Not to be unfairly dismissed

See chapter 5.

Notice of termination of employment

The minimum notice periods for termination of employment are as follows:

By the employer:

Length of employee's service	*Minimum notice period*
Less than 1 month	Nil
1 month–2 years	1 week
2–3 years	2 weeks

…and an additional week for each year of continuous employment to a maximum of 12 weeks.

By the employee: one week.

> **?** **I want to quit my job, what's the minimum notice I have to give my boss?**
>
> *One week.*

Protected rights on the transfer of a trade or business

When a trade or business is transferred from one employer to another, its employees automatically become employees of the new employer, as if their contract of employment were originally made with the new employer. The service is counted as continuous from the date on which the employment began with the first employer.

Redundancy pay

See chapter 5.

Remuneration on suspension on medical grounds

You are entitled to be paid for up to 26 weeks if, in compliance with any regulation or law that concerns the health and safety of workers, you are suspended on medical grounds.

You are entitled to be paid 'a week's pay' (or a proportion of 'a week's pay') for every week of suspension. If you want an explanation of how to calculate a week's pay, see the Department of Trade and Industry's (DTI's) booklet entitled 'Rules Governing Continuous Employment and a Week's Pay' (see 'Useful contacts' section).

You can complain to an employment tribunal about your employer's failure to make a medical suspension payment within three months of the day on which it is alleged that payment was not made. The tribunal will extend the time limit for bringing the claim if it was not reasonably practicable for the claim to be made within three months.

Statutory Sick Pay

Subject to satisfying certain conditions, you are entitled to receive Statutory Sick Pay (SSP) from your employer when you are absent from work because of sickness. The current weekly rate of SSP is £68.20, verifiable by contacting the Department for Work and Pensions (DWP) or the Advisory Conciliation and Arbitration Service (ACAS) (see 'Useful contacts' section). This sum is subject to Income Tax and National Insurance contributions.

Unless the contract of employment states that there is a right to be paid normal pay for a period of sickness absence, SSP is all the employer is obliged to pay an employee during sickness.

You are not eligible for SSP if on the first day of sickness:

- you are aged under 16 or over 65;

- you have a contract of services which is for a specified period of three months or less;

- your average weekly pay is below the point at which National Insurance contributions are payable (currently £82);

- you have received Social Security Benefit in the 57 days before the first day of sickness;

- you have not yet started working;

- you become sick while pregnant during the Statutory Maternity Pay period;

- you have been due SSP for 28 weeks from a former employer and the last day on which SSP was paid is eight weeks ago or less;

- you become sick during a trade dispute at your workplace, unless you can prove you have no direct interest in the dispute; or

- you are in legal custody.

If notified that an ineligible employee has been absent for four or more consecutive days, your employer must send a form to you within seven days that explains why SSP is not payable. You may then claim Incapacity Benefit. Forms for claiming Incapacity Benefit are available from local Jobcentre Plus offices.

SSP is only payable:

- if you have been incapable of work for four or more consecutive days; and

- if you have notified your employer of your absence and given evidence of your incapacity, i.e. a doctor's note (in accordance with any rules laid down by your employer which must be made available to all employees); and

- for days on which you would normally be required to work; and

- until:

    (i) you return to work; or

(ii) SSP has been paid for 28 weeks (if you are still sick in these circumstances, you shall become entitled to Incapacity Benefit); or

(iii) the expiry or termination of your contract of employment; or

(iv) you become entitled to Maternity Allowance or Statutory Maternity Pay (see chapter 3); or

(v) you go into legal custody.

If there are less than eight weeks between any periods of absence, they're linked and counted as one period of absence for SSP purposes.

Employers must issue a Form SSP(I)(T) to employees whose maximum entitlement to 28 weeks is about to expire, no later than the 23rd week of sickness.

Sunday shop working

Unless you are employed to work only on Sundays, if you are employed as a shop worker you have protection from dismissal, selection for redundancy or any other disadvantage for refusing to work on Sundays.

Even if you have agreed to work on Sundays, you can opt out of Sunday working by giving your employer three months' notice. Your employer should have given you a written explanatory statement setting out your right to opt out and if it fails to do so within two months of you agreeing to work on Sundays, the opt-out notice period is reduced from three months to one month.

Time off

Holiday

All workers have the right to the minimum of 20 days' paid holiday per year. Paid public holidays (of which there are currently eight in the UK) can be counted as part of the statutory 20 days' holiday entitlement. Some employers provide more generous contractual holiday entitlement than the statutory minimum.

> **?** **My employer counts Bank Holidays as part of my holiday allowance, can he do that?**
>
> *Yes, they can be counted as part of your statutory 20 days' holiday.*

If you are a part-time worker, you are entitled to the same holidays as a full-time worker, calculated on a pro rata basis. So, for example, where your employer gives full-time employees 20 days' holiday per year (plus public holidays), if you work three days a week (Tuesday to Thursday) you should have 12 days' paid holiday (plus 3/5 of the year's public holidays even if you do not work on Mondays).

You cannot carry holiday time over into the following year, nor can you receive payment in lieu to replace unused holiday time, except where your employment is terminated. Some contracts of employment allow some holiday to be carried over or to attract payment in lieu; this is acceptable provided it is holiday that exceeds the statutory minimum holiday entitlement.

> Point of Law
>
> *Working Time Regulations 1998*

You are entitled to be paid for each week of your statutory leave entitlement. This is relatively easy to calculate if your pay does not vary with the amount of work done. However, if your pay varies with the amount of work done or you are a shift or rota worker or if you have no normal working hours, then the amount of a week's pay is the average pay received over the preceding 12 weeks.

Public duties

You are entitled to time off to perform the public duties listed below. The amount of time you can take depends upon your employer's business and the effect of your absence.

- As a justice of the peace.

- As a member of a local authority.

- As a member of the Broads Authority (an authority with responsibilities for conservation and recreation on the Norfolk Broads).

- As a member of any statutory tribunal.

- As a member of a board of visitors or a visiting committee.

- As a member of a National Health Service trust, a Regional Health Authority, an Area Health Authority, a District Health Authority, a Family Practitioner Committee or a Health Board.

- As a member of the managing or governing body of an educational establishment maintained by a local education authority or a school council or the governing body of a designated institution or a central institution.

- As a member of the governing body of a grant-maintained school.

- As a member of the governing body of a further education corporation or higher education corporation.

- As a member of a school board or of the board of management of a self-governing school.

- As a member of the board of management of a college of further education.

- As a member of the National Rivers Authority or a river purification board.

There is no right to have time off for jury service or to attend court as a witness. But an employer who prevents such attendance would be in contempt of court.

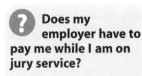

? Does my employer have to pay me while I am on jury service?

No, but you can claim an allowance from the court.

There is no automatic right to be paid by your employer while on jury service. You can claim an allowance from the court for loss of earnings (up to a cap), travel costs and a subsistence rate. For details of the rates payable, see the Court Service website (www.courtservice.gov.uk).

Trade union activities, duties and training

Officials of independent trade unions are entitled to time off with pay to perform duties concerned with the industrial relations in the employing company and to undergo training. There is also a right to time off to accompany another worker at disciplinary and grievance hearings.

Union members are entitled to time off without pay in order to take part in trade union activities (e.g. voting in a union election, recruiting new members, distributing union literature and attending branch meetings).

Elected employee representatives

If you are an employee who has been elected as an employee representative for consultation purposes regarding collective redundancies or the transfer of a trade or business, you are entitled to reasonable paid time off to perform your functions as a representative. You also have the right to paid leave to undergo training.

Safety representatives

Safety representatives appointed by recognised trade unions are entitled to paid time off during working time to carry out their functions and undergo training for these functions. Representatives of non-unionised workplaces are also entitled to paid time off to carry out functions and undergo training.

Pension scheme trustees

If you are a pension scheme trustee, you are entitled to paid time off during working hours for performing your duties or for training in connection with those duties.

Maternity leave, including antenatal care

See chapter 3.

Redundancy

See chapter 5.

Parental leave

See chapter 3.

Paternity leave

See chapter 3.

Time off for dependants

See chapter 3.

Working time

Subject to certain exceptions, you cannot be required to work more than 48 hours per week unless you agree to opt out of the 48-hour limit.

Point of Law
Working Time Regulations 1998

Any agreement to opt out of this 48-hour limit must be in writing and you must not be forced to opt out or suffer any disadvantage if you refuse to opt out.

You are also entitled to:

- frequent short breaks if your work is monotonous or your work rate is predetermined;

- 20 minutes' rest every six hours if the working day is longer than six hours;

- 11 consecutive hours' rest in any 24-hour period;

- 24 consecutive hours' rest in every seven-day period.

If you work nights, you cannot be required to work more than eight hours in 24. This working time can be averaged

> **? I work nights and my health is suffering, what can I do?**
>
> *You should ask your employer to give you a free health check.*

over 17 weeks unless you are involved in special hazards or heavy physical/mental strain, when no averaging is allowed. If you work nights, you are also entitled to free health assessments before you start the position and then at regular intervals. If your GP certifies that you are suffering from health problems connected with night work, you may transfer to alternative day work.

Written reasons for dismissal (upon request)

If you are dismissed and you have one year's continuous service, you can ask your employer for a written statement of reasons for dismissal. If the statement is not provided within 14 days, or if the reasons given are inadequate or untrue, you can complain to an employment tribunal and claim compensation of two weeks' pay.

Written statement of terms and conditions of employment

You have a right to be provided with a written statement of the terms and conditions of your employment, unless your employment is for a period of less than one month. This is called the 'principal statement' and is often covered by your contract.

If you are employed for more than 13 weeks, you may complain to an employment tribunal if your employer fails to provide the written statement of the terms of employment.

Information which must be included in the principal statement:

- The names of the parties.

- The date on which employment began and the date on which any previous employment (with this or any other employer) commenced which is to be regarded as continuous with this employment.

- The scale or rate of remuneration or the method of calculating such remuneration and the frequency of payment.

- Any terms and conditions relating to hours of work, including normal working hours.

- Any terms and conditions relating to entitlement to holidays, including public holidays and holiday pay (enough to enable your entitlement, including entitlement to accrued holiday pay on termination, to be precisely calculated).

- Your job title or a brief description of your work.

- Your place of work, or if you are required or permitted to work at various places, an indication of that fact, together with the address of your employer.

Information which must be given in writing (e.g in a separate letter), but which may or may not be included in the principal statement (even when there are no such arrangements under these, this fact should be stated):

- Where the job is not intended to be permanent, the period for which it is expected to continue.

- Where the job is for a fixed term, the expiry date.

- The length of notice you are obliged to give and are entitled to receive in order to terminate your contract (or reference to the law or an accessible collective agreement, i.e. one negotiated between your employer and your trade union).

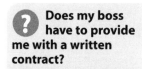

Does my boss have to provide me with a written contract?

Strictly speaking, no; but written terms and conditions must be provided if your job lasts for more than a month.

- The rules relating to sick leave and sick pay (or reference to a document where such details may be found).

- Any collective agreements which directly affect your terms and conditions of employment including, where your employer is not a party, the names of the parties.

- The details of any pensions or pension schemes (or reference to documents where such details may be found).

- A statement of whether a State Pension contracting-out certificate is or is not in force.

- Where you are required to work outside the UK for more than one month, the period of such service, the currency in which remuneration will be paid, and additional remuneration and/or benefits provided while working overseas and any terms and conditions of employment relating to your return to the UK.

- Any disciplinary rules and grievance procedures applying to you (or reference to documents where these details can be found). This only applies if your employer employs more than 20 employees.

- The person to whom you can complain if you have any grievances or you are dissatisfied with a disciplinary decision (or reference to documents where these details can be found).

Statutory dispute resolution procedures

All employers are required to apply certain procedures when dealing with disciplinary or dismissal situations. Employees also have to take certain steps to try to resolve their grievances with their employer before bringing a claim in an employment tribunal.

Whenever an employer is contemplating dismissing an employee or taking disciplinary action other than giving a warning (e.g. demotion or transferring him to work in a different department) it must follow the standard dismissal and disciplinary procedure.

The main consequence of a failure by an employer to follow the procedures is that dismissal will be deemed to be automatically unfair (subject to the employee having a year's service) and the compensatory award may be increased or decreased by between 10 to 50 per cent, depending on which party is at fault (subject to the statutory cap of £56,800). For further details on unfair dismissal and automatically unfair dismissal, see chapter 5.

If you have a grievance about an action by your employer, you will need to initiate the statutory grievance procedure before you can bring a subsequent employment tribunal claim.

Can I rely on verbal promises made by my employer during my interview, or during my employment as forming part of my contract of employment?

The terms of your contract can be written or verbal. The difficulty with relying on verbal promises as contractual terms is that they are very much more difficult to prove; it will often be your word against your employer's. This can be particularly difficult if a period of time has passed since your job started and memories have faded, or if the relevant manager who made the verbal promise has left your employer. Therefore, if a verbal promise has been made and you wish to rely on this as a contractual term, it is wise to ask your employer to incorporate it into your contract.

Before agreeing to any written contract of employment it is sensible to ensure that all of the benefits you have been verbally promised are included in the contract.

Can my employer change the terms of my contract?

Generally, your employer cannot change the terms of your contract without first obtaining your agreement.

However, there are some changes that your employer can make if it built 'flexibility' into your contract, for example, by stating that 'You may be required to work anywhere in the

UK' or that 'You will work eight hours in 24, day, night or shift work'.

Another way flexibility may have been built into your contract is by the use of terms that can be altered or removed. For example, entitlement to a bonus may be stated to be at your manager's discretion and/or your employer may reserve the right to remove entitlement to a bonus without compensation.

> **? I have been asked to start work an hour earlier, must I comply?**
>
> *Not unless your contract or staff handbook states that your hours of work may be changed.*

A staff handbook 'as issued from time to time' may be stated to be incorporated into a contract. This would mean that matters dealt with in a handbook could be changed and that change would be automatically incorporated into the contract, without the need of your employee's express consent.

If the contract contains such flexibility, then your employer will be able to alter the terms in line with these clauses provided it introduces the changes in a reasonable manner. For example, if a mobility clause is included in the contract, your employer should give reasonable notice before requiring you to relocate.

If there is no flexibility, then your employer must follow the correct procedure if it wants to alter your terms of employment. Your employer must offer the new terms to you; you can either accept or reject them. If you do nothing, this does not mean you have accepted the new terms. The only time doing nothing can amount to acceptance is when your employer's letter varying the terms says something like 'If you do not object in writing within 14 days you will be deemed to have accepted the change'. Alternatively, it is possible for you to accept the new terms by your conduct; if you change your behaviour to comply with a term in the offer (e.g. you turn up for work at a new time), you will be judged to have accepted the new terms.

If you do not accept the changes, your employer may dismiss you and then offer employment on the new terms. However, if this happens you may have a claim for breach of contract, unfair dismissal or redundancy if the correct procedures are not followed and fair reasons for dismissal do not exist (see chapter 5 for further details on termination of employment).

CHAPTER 3

Family-friendly rights

As an employee you have some important rights in relation to your family. Some employers give their employees enhanced family-friendly rights in their contracts or in a staff handbook, but all employers must give you the following as a minimum.

Maternity rights

These are the main rights that a female employee who is expecting a baby has:

- Time off for antenatal care

- Suspension from work on maternity grounds

- The right to take maternity leave and return to work

- Statutory Maternity Pay

- Protection from dismissal and detrimental treatment

Time off for antenatal care

If you are pregnant, you are entitled to paid time off for antenatal care, irrespective of your length of service or the number of hours worked. Husbands or partners of pregnant women have no statutory right to attend antenatal appointments. Except in the case of the first appointment, you must produce a certificate confirming your pregnancy and an appointment card or some other document showing that an appointment has been made, if requested to do so by your employer.

The length of absence must be reasonable. It may include time for travelling to and from an appointment. If an appointment lasts longer than expected, your employer should still pay you for the whole of the time that was required to attend the appointment. However, you should not abuse your right by taking more time off than is necessary.

It may be reasonable for an employer to refuse you time off if you can arrange to have the antenatal care outside your normal working hours (e.g. if you work part-time or shifts). However, the timing of appointments is often outside an individual's control and, if this is so, your employer may not refuse you time off for antenatal care during your working hours. Your employer cannot require you to make up the time later.

What care is included in the right?

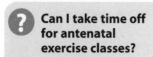

? Can I take time off for antenatal exercise classes?

Yes, as long as your healthcare adviser recommends it.

Antenatal care on the advice of a registered medical practitioner, midwife or health visitor is covered. The number of visits required and the length of each visit depend on your medical condition. Exercise and relaxation classes are also covered if they are on the recommendation of your medical advisers.

You have no right to be paid for time off for infertility treatment. However, if you become pregnant as a result of it, then you enjoy the same right to paid time off for antenatal care as any other pregnant employee. It is likely that you would need more time off work for antenatal care and your employer would be obliged to allow you the time off as it would probably be considered reasonable.

Doctors' appointments to ascertain whether or not you are pregnant would probably be regarded as antenatal care only if you turned out to be pregnant.

Pay entitlement

You should be paid your normal hourly rate of pay by your employer during the period of time off for antenatal care. If you are paid on the basis of a fixed salary, you should be paid as normal. If you are paid by the hours you work, the rate of pay is calculated by dividing the amount of one week's pay by the normal working hours in a week. If the number of hours worked per week is irregular, they should be averaged over the previous 12 complete working weeks.

Remedies

You would be guilty of misconduct if you took time off without authorisation, but you can complain to an employment tribunal if your employer unreasonably refuses to give you time off or does not pay you for the time you have taken off.

Suspension from work on maternity grounds

Point of Law

Employment Rights Act 1996

Your employer has an obligation to carry out risk assessments for the safety of its employees including any risk posed to the health and safety of women who are of childbearing age.

If there is a risk to you, your employer must take preventative or protective action by varying your working conditions or hours of work or by offering any suitable alternative work. If no alternative work is available, your employer has a duty to suspend you from work with pay for as long as necessary to avoid the risk.

You have these rights regardless of your length of service or the number of hours that you work. However, to be entitled to these rights you must notify your employer in writing that you are pregnant or have given birth within the previous six months or are breastfeeding.

The right to take maternity leave and return to work

If you are expecting a baby, you are entitled to 26 weeks' 'ordinary maternity leave', regardless of your length of service or hours of work and a further 26 weeks' 'additional maternity leave' subject to having sufficient service as described below.

> **Point of Law**
>
> *Maternity and Parental Leave etc Regulations 1999*

Quite often an employer does offer employees more favourable maternity provisions than the statutory rights, so it is worth checking your contract and/or staff handbook for these.

These rights to ordinary maternity leave and additional maternity leave apply where a woman gives birth to a living child or has a stillbirth after 24 weeks of pregnancy.

Ordinary maternity leave

Duration

Maternity leave may not begin before the start of the 11th week before the beginning of the week in which the baby is due. Subject to this, maternity leave begins on the date you tell your employer you intend your leave to start.

Maternity leave can begin earlier than the date you choose if you are absent from work for a reason that is wholly or partly because of your pregnancy. The Department for Work and Pensions publishes a free leaflet, 'Pregnancy Related Illnesses', NI200, which sets out the illnesses that are recognised as being connected to pregnancy. In these circumstances, your maternity leave shall begin on the first day of your absence, provided that date is after the beginning of the sixth week before the start of the week the baby is due.

Women are prohibited from working within two weeks of childbirth; it is a criminal offence for your employer to fail to comply with this prohibition.

Notification

You are only entitled to maternity leave if you give the required notice of:

- the fact that you are pregnant;

- the expected week your baby is due (or the date of the birth in the unlikely event that it has already occurred); and

- the date you wish your leave to begin.

Notification must be given by your 26th week of pregnancy or, if that is not possible, as soon as is reasonably practicable after that. If your employer asks for one, you must produce a certificate from a registered medical practitioner or midwife stating the expected week the baby is due.

If the maternity leave period has started before the notified leave date, either because of a pregnancy-related absence or because you have given birth, you must notify your employer as soon as

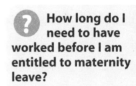

? How long do I need to have worked before I am entitled to maternity leave?

There is no minimum period.

you can. If your employer asks for it, this notification must be in writing. Once your employer has received notification from you as set out above, it must write to you within 28 days to inform you of the date your maternity leave will end.

Rights during ordinary maternity leave

The contract of employment continues and you are entitled to continue to receive all of your usual benefits except wages and salary (but including benefits in kind).

Additional maternity leave

You are entitled to additional maternity leave if you have 26 weeks' continuous service by your 26th week of pregnancy.

Duration

Additional maternity leave may last for up to 26 weeks beginning at the end of the ordinary maternity leave period. In other words, if you take ordinary and additional maternity leave you will be off work for 52 weeks.

Notification

No notice needs to be given by you of your intentions to take additional maternity leave; it is presumed you will take it unless you notify otherwise.

Rights during additional maternity leave

The contract of employment continues, but there is no statutory right to pay and benefits during the additional maternity leave period. Your obligation of good faith continues during this period, so you may not work elsewhere in breach of this duty.

Right to return to work

Ordinary maternity leave

If you return after 26 weeks' maternity leave, you normally have the right to return to the same job that you left. If the job that you left was full-time and you would prefer to work in a more flexible way, you may request flexible working (see later in this chapter for more details). If you want to return to work before the end of your 26-week leave, you must give your employer at least 28 days' notice of the date you intend to return to work.

Additional maternity leave

If you return after additional maternity leave, you normally have the right to return to the same job that you left. If that is not reasonably practicable, you may be offered another job that is both suitable and appropriate in the circumstances. In either case, you must be offered terms and conditions that are no less favourable than those which would have applied had you not been absent from work.

Statutory Maternity Pay

Subject to qualifying for payment (see below), you are entitled to Statutory Maternity Pay (SMP) even if you do not intend to return to work after the child is born.

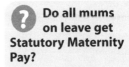

Do all mums on leave get Statutory Maternity Pay?

No, you must satisfy certain conditions.

Eligibility

As a mother or prospective mother, you only qualify for SMP if:

- you have stopped work wholly or partly because of pregnancy or childbirth; and

- you have 26 weeks' continuous employment with the same employer by the 26th week of pregnancy; and

- your normal weekly earnings in the eight weeks before the 26th week of pregnancy were above the lower earnings limit for the payment of National Insurance contributions (currently £82) (if your normal weekly earnings are below the lower earnings limit, you can apply for Maternity Allowance from the DSS on Form SMP1); and

- you have reached the start of the 11th week before the expected week of childbirth (or you have given birth before that date).

Entitlement

You are entitled to SMP for 26 weeks as follows:

- for six weeks, 90 per cent of your normal weekly earnings (over a reference period of eight weeks immediately before the 26th week of pregnancy); and

- for 20 weeks thereafter, at a current flat rate of £106 per week.

SMP is subject to Income Tax, National Insurance contributions and any other regular deductions. SMP should be paid by the same method and at the same time that you would normally be paid. If there is no normal agreement as to which day wages are paid on, payment should be made on the last day of the calendar month.

SMP must be calculated, or adjusted, to take account of any salary increase received between the start of the reference period and the end of the period when you are in receipt of the higher rate of SMP.

If you have a contractual right to maternity pay, your employer may offset this against SMP.

If your employer fails to pay SMP or you dispute the amount paid, you should ask your employer for a written statement of what SMP it considers to be due and the reasons why. If nothing is resolved, the matter may be referred to an adjudication officer. An appeal regarding the adjudication officer's decision may be made to the Social Security Appeals Tribunal and a further appeal may be put forward, on a point of law only, to the Social Security Commissioners.

Protection from dismissal and detrimental treatment

Dismissal or selection for redundancy of any woman who is pregnant, or has recently given birth, is automatically unfair, regardless of her length of service or hours of work, if the reason or principal reason for dismissal is maternity/ pregnancy related. For further details see chapter 5.

A dismissal by reason of pregnancy may also amount to direct discrimination on the ground of sex (see chapter 4).

You must also not be subjected to any disadvantage (e.g. a reduction of salary or benefits, or lack of promotion (when this is warranted)) for any maternity- or pregnancy-related reason. No qualifying period of work is required and you can seek compensation through an employment tribunal.

If you are dismissed at any time during your pregnancy or maternity period, you are entitled to written reasons for your dismissal, regardless of length of service, without having to make a request for written reasons. You may raise a complaint with an employment tribunal if you are not provided with written reasons for your dismissal and if the complaint is well founded the employment tribunal may award you a sum equivalent to two weeks' pay.

Adoption rights

Point of Law

Employment Rights Act 1996
Paternity and Adoption Leave
Regulations 2002

The statutory adoption rights described below apply to both male and female employees; they mirror, as closely as possible, the provisions for maternity rights. Some employers may offer more favourable adoption provisions than the statutory rights, so it is worth checking the contract and any staff handbook for these.

The right to take adoption leave

If you satisfy the following conditions, you will have the right to take ordinary adoption leave of 26 weeks and additional adoption leave of a further 26 weeks. You must:

- have been matched by an adoption agency with a child;

- have at least 26 weeks' continuous service by the week you are notified of the match;

- be legally adopting the child;

- have given proper notice to your employer of your intention to take leave;

- have provided your employer with evidence of your entitlement to take adoption leave.

> **?** **Can my husband and I both take adoption leave?**
>
> *No, statutory adoption leave is only available to one of you.*

Adoption leave is not available where the child is already known to the adopters (e.g. in step-family adoptions or adoptions by existing foster carers).

If a couple are jointly adopting a child, only one partner will be able to take adoption leave. You should give written notice of your plans to take ordinary adoption leave within seven days of having been notified of a match, unless this is not reasonably practicable. The notice must specify:

* the expected date of placement;

* the date on which the leave will commence.

You must also provide your employer with a letter issued by the matching adoption agency stating:

* the name and address of the agency;

* your name and address;

* the date on which the employee was first notified of the match; and

* the date on which the agency expects to place the child.

Your employer should then respond to you in writing with the date that your adoption leave will end.

Rights during adoption leave and the right to return to work

These rights mirror the provisions for maternity rights discussed earlier in this chapter.

Protection from dismissal and detrimental treatment

Dismissal or selection for redundancy of any employee who took or sought to take adoption leave is automatically unfair, regardless of length of service or hours of work. However, there is an exemption for small companies employing fewer than five employees where it is not reasonably practicable to allow the employee on adoption leave to return to a job which is both suitable and appropriate. There is no similar exemption in maternity legislation.

Statutory Adoption Pay

Subject to qualifying for payment (see below), you are entitled to Statutory Adoption Pay (SAP) even if you do not intend to return to work after taking adoption leave.

Eligibility

You only qualify for SAP if:

- you have stopped work because of adoption leave;

- you have 26 weeks' continuous employment with the same employer by the date you have been notified of the match;

- you are a person with whom a child is, or is expected to be, placed for adoption;

- you have normal weekly earnings of above the lower earnings limit for the payment of National Insurance contributions (currently £82);

- you have not elected to receive Statutory Paternity Pay (discussed later in this chapter).

Entitlement

The employee is entitled to SAP for 26 weeks at the current standard rate of £106 per week (or 90 per cent of average weekly earnings if this is less than £106 per week).

SAP is subject to Income Tax, National Insurance contributions and any other regular deductions. The rules for payment of SAP mirror those for SMP.

Parental leave

Point of Law
Employment Rights Act 1996

You can take 13 weeks' unpaid leave for the purpose of caring for a child subject to satisfying certain qualifying conditions. Parents of a child who is entitled to a Disability Living Allowance have a right to take 18 weeks' unpaid leave.

Qualifying conditions

To qualify for parental leave you must:

- have one year's service; and

- have or expect to have responsibility for a child, by:

  - being the natural father or mother, married at the time of birth.

  - being the natural mother where you and the father were not married at the time of birth.

  - being the natural father where you and the mother were not married at the time of birth, if you as the father acquire parental responsibility by court order or by agreement with the mother.

  - being a legal guardian.

  - being an adoptive parent.

The child must have been under five on 15 December 1999 or if the child is an adopted child, the child must have been adopted after 15 December 1994.

 Who may take parental leave?

Subject to certain conditions, both parents can take up to a total of 13 weeks off, unpaid, to look after a child.

The right to parental leave is an individual one and will be non-transferable. This means that both parents will be able to take up to 13 weeks' leave if they are both working, but they will not be able to add their leave entitlement so that one of them can take more than 13 weeks and the other less.

When can parental leave be taken?

Parental leave may be taken before the child's fifth birthday or where the child has been adopted, for a period of five years or up to the age of 18, whichever is the sooner. An exception to this is where your employer has postponed parental leave (see below); in such circumstances it would be possible to have the postponed leave taken after the fifth birthday or anniversary of the adoption cut-off point.

Where a child is entitled to a Disability Living Allowance, parental leave may be taken at any time up to the child's 18th birthday.

Parental leave may not be taken in periods of less than a week and any fraction of a week will be treated as a whole week. The exception is in cases where the child is entitled to a Disability Living Allowance. Unless your employer agrees otherwise, you may not take more than four weeks' parental leave in respect of any individual child during a 12-month period.

Notification

To take parental leave you must give your employer 21 days' notice. When leave is due to start on the birth of a child or the placement of a child for adoption, the notice needs to be given at least 21 days before the beginning of the expected week of childbirth or week of placement. Notification requirements may differ if your employer has agreed its own parental leave scheme by way of collective bargaining or a workforce agreement.

Postponement of parental leave

Your employer can postpone when a period of parental leave may be taken, except where it is to be taken on the birth or adoption of a child. In every other circumstance, your employer can postpone parental leave if it considers that the operation of the business would be unduly disrupted. Your employer must agree to allow you to take the same period of leave within six months. To postpone, your employer must give notice within seven days after receipt of your notice requesting leave.

Rights during parental leave

The employment relationship continues during the leave period, although leave may be unpaid. The employment relationship continues in exactly the same way as in the case of a person taking additional maternity leave, namely, you are entitled to the benefit of your employer's implied obligation to you of trust and confidence and you are also bound by your implied obligation of good faith and any expressed obligation prohibiting disclosure of confidential information or your participation in any competing business.

Right to return to work

If you take parental leave for a period of more than four weeks or immediately after additional maternity leave, you have the right to return to your old job at the end of the leave period. Alternatively, if it is not reasonably feasible for you to return to your old job, you have the right to return to another job which is both suitable for you and appropriate in the circumstances. You may return to work after parental leave on terms no less favourable than those which would have been applicable to you had you not been absent from work.

Enforcement

You have a right to make a claim in the employment tribunal if your employer unreasonably postpones, or refuses, or attempts to prevent, the grant of parental leave. The tribunal will award compensation as it thinks fit, taking into account your employer's behaviour and the loss sustained by you.

You also have protection from being subjected to any disadvantage because you took or tried to take parental leave. If you are dismissed for a reason relating to the fact that you took parental leave, dismissal is automatically unfair. See chapter 5 for more on termination.

Time off for dependants

> **Point of Law**
>
> *Employment Rights Act 1996*

All employees (regardless of length of service) may take a reasonable amount of unpaid leave to deal with incidents involving a dependant. Dependants include your parents, wife, husband or partner, child or someone who lives as part of the family.

You have the right to time off:

- to help when a dependant is ill or injured;

- to cope when the arrangements for caring for a dependant unexpectedly break down;

- when a dependant gives birth;

- when a dependant dies; or

- to deal with an unexpected incident involving a dependent child during school hours or on a school trip.

In the first two cases, the dependant could also be someone who relies on you in a particular emergency (such as your neighbour).

The length of time that you need to take will depend on the circumstances, but it is only a right to assist temporarily with the dependant and not to provide longer-term care. For example, if your childcare arrangements

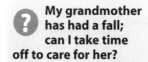

My grandmother has had a fall; can I take time off to care for her?

Yes, but it can be unpaid and can only be taken to make arrangements for someone else to care for her.

unexpectedly break down because your childminder resigns, you can take unpaid time off to care for your child and find alternative arrangements. One or two days will usually be the most that are needed to deal with the immediate issues and to sort out longer-term arrangements if necessary.

You may complain to an employment tribunal if your employer unreasonably refuses you permission to take time off for dependants. If the tribunal finds the complaint well-founded, the tribunal will award compensation as it thinks fit, having considered your employer's fault and any loss sustained by you.

Employees also have protection from any disadvantage because they took or sought to take time off for dependants.

Paternity rights

Paternity leave

Point of Law
Employment Rights Act 1996
Paternity and Adoption Leave
Regulations 2002

People mistakenly think that paternity leave is only available for men. However, in the case of same-sex female partners, paternity leave may be available to a female employee who has an 'enduring relationship' with the child's mother. Any employee who satisfies the following conditions as to an expected child will have the right to take paternity leave. The employee must:

- have at least 26 weeks' continuous service by the beginning of the 14th week before the expected week for childbirth or in the case of an adopted child, by the beginning of the week the adopter is notified of being matched with the child;

- have a relationship with the child;

- be the biological father of the child or be married to or have an enduring relationship with the child's mother.

Notification

If you wish to take paternity leave you must give notice of:

> **Paternity leave is for dads, right?**
>
> *Not always. A woman who is the long-term partner of a child's mother can also qualify.*

- the expected week of childbirth, or if the birth has already occurred, the actual date of the child's birth, or the date of placement if the child is adopted;

- the period of leave to be taken (which may be in one block of either one or two weeks); and

- the date on which the leave will begin.

Paternity leave must be taken within 56 days of the expected week of childbirth or placement.

Rights during paternity leave and the right to return to work

These rights mirror the provisions for ordinary maternity leave. Please note that the same exemption that applies for small companies in relation to adoption leave applies here.

Statutory Paternity Pay

Subject to qualifying for payments (see below), you are entitled to Statutory Paternity Pay (SPP) even if you do not intend to work after the child is born/adopted.

Eligibility and entitlement

You shall qualify for SPP (which is currently at the rate of £106 per week) if:

- you have a right to take paternity leave;

- you have normal weekly earnings that are above the lower earnings limit for the payment of National Insurance contributions (currently £82);

- you give at least 28 days' notice (unless this is not reasonably practicable) of the date from which you expect SPP to be paid; and

- you have completed a self-declaration that you are entitled to receive SPP.

Flexible working

Point of Law

Flexible Working (Eligibility, Complaints and Remedies) Regulations 2002
Flexible Working (Procedural Requirements) Regulations 2002

Certain employees (men or women) have the statutory right to make a request to adopt flexible working arrangements to care for a child, such as working part-time or from home. This is *not* a right to work flexibly, simply a right to *make a request* and to have the request properly considered.

Eligibility

To be eligible to make such a request you must:

- have a child under six, or if a child is disabled, under 18 years; and

- have been continuously employed for at least 26 weeks at the date of making the request; and

- be making the request to enable you to care for the child; and

- have responsibility or expect to have responsibility for the child; and

- be a biological parent, guardian, adopter or foster carer of the child; or

- be married to or be the partner of and/or live with the biological parent, guardian, adopter or foster carer of the child; and

- not have made another application to work flexibly in the past 12 months.

Making an application

If you make an application to work flexibly, you must do so in writing, stating:

- that the application is being made under the statutory right to request a flexible working pattern; and

- that you have responsibility for the upbringing of the child and you are either the mother, father, adopter, guardian or foster parent, or are married to, or are the partner of, the child's mother, father, adopter, guardian or foster parent;

- the flexible working pattern you are applying for and the date you would like it to become effective;

- what effect, if any, you think the proposed change will have on your employer and how, in your opinion, any such effect may be dealt with; and

- whether a previous application has been made to your employer and, if so, when it was made.

Considering the application

Your employer must consider any request by you to work flexibly and within 28 days it must hold a meeting with you to discuss the application and any possible compromises.

 Do I have an automatic right to work flexitime?

No, you have to qualify and then you only have the right to ask for flexitime and have your request considered.

You may be accompanied at this meeting by a fellow worker, a full-time trade union official or a lay union official of your choice. Your employer must notify you of its decision within a further 14 days.

If your employer accepts the application, unless the parties agree otherwise, the new working arrangements will be permanent and you have no right to revert to your old working conditions. Therefore, if you only want the new arrangements to continue for a set period while your child is very young, for example, you should try to agree this with your employer. In any event, the parties will need to discuss what arrangements will need to be made for when the working pattern is changed and it is likely that your employer will issue a revised contract reflecting changes in hours/pay and any other terms.

Your employer may refuse the request if it has a clear business reason. The business grounds for refusing an application must be from one of those listed below:

- Burden of additional costs.
- Detrimental effect on ability to meet customer demand.
- Inability to reorganise work among existing staff.
- Inability to recruit additional staff.
- Detrimental impact on quality.
- Detrimental impact on performance.
- Insufficiency of work during the work period proposed.
- Planned structural changes.

Your employer must give a full explanation of why it is refusing the request.

Appeal

Once your employer has given its decision, if you are unhappy with it, you have 14 days to appeal in writing. Your employer must arrange an appeal meeting to take place within 14 days. You may be accompanied at the appeal meeting by a fellow worker, full-time trade union official or lay union official of your choice. Following the appeal meeting, you must be informed of the outcome of the appeal in writing within 14 days.

Remedies

You can complain to an employment tribunal on the grounds that your employer has:

- failed to comply with its statutory duties in relation to your application to work flexibly; or

- based its decision to reject the application on incorrect facts.

You must first exhaust your employer's appeal process. You must make the complaint within three months of either the date on which you were notified of the appeal decision or the date on which the alleged breach of your employer's duty was committed.

The tribunal does not have the power to order an employer to implement a flexible working arrangement so a claim on this basis is of little assistance to you. However, claims under discrimination legislation can still be brought. Therefore, a female employee returning from maternity leave and being refused the right to work part-time, for example, may still have a valid claim for indirect sex discrimination (see chapter 4 for further details on discrimination).

CHAPTER 4

Discrimination

As an employee, you have a high level of protection from discrimination and you do not need a qualifying period of employment in order to bring such a claim. What is more, discrimination claims are not subject to any maximum compensation award.

Point of Law

Disability Act 1995
Employment Equality (Religion or Belief) Regulations 2003
Employment Equality (Sexual Orientation) Regulations 2003
Equal Pay Act 1970
Race Relations Act 1976
Sex Discrimination Act 1975

There is currently protection from discrimination in relation to sex, gender reassignment (i.e. 'sex change'), marital status, race, disability, sexual orientation and religion or religious belief. Common themes run through all of these areas of discrimination and these are described in this chapter. There are also some points that are specific to a particular form of discrimination or where the common theme does not apply and these are also pointed out. Unequal treatment on the ground of sex is also protected by the law on equal pay that is also covered in this chapter.

Common themes

Discrimination is forbidden at every stage of employment (i.e. advertising vacancies, hiring of employees, promotion, training and other opportunities, and dismissal).

Your Rights at Work

There are four recognised forms of discrimination:

(i) **Direct discrimination**

(ii) **Indirect discrimination**

(iii) **Harassment**

(iv) **Victimisation**

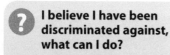

I believe I have been discriminated against, what can I do?

As a first step, contact employment tribunal central enquiries.

Generally, in judging whether you have been discriminated against, you need to compare how you and someone else with similar skills and qualifications have been treated. The intention or motive of the alleged discriminator is irrelevant.

Direct discrimination

Direct discrimination is easy to recognise: it occurs if you have received less favourable treatment because of your sex, marital status, race, gender reassignment, disability, sexual orientation, religion or religious belief.

An individual may exercise unconscious prejudices because of upbringing and perceptions without being aware of the fact. All the same, this can amount to direct discrimination.

In order to succeed in an employment tribunal with a complaint of discrimination, you would only need to bring evidence that would simply lead the tribunal to presume or infer (not conclude) that there had been discrimination. It would then be up to your employer to disprove this presumption or inference. If your employer could not disprove it and there was a finding of direct discrimination, no question of justification for your employer's treatment could arise. The exception to this is in relation to disability discrimination (see below).

Sex discrimination – maternity cases

Unfavourable treatment on the grounds of an employee's pregnancy or other maternity-related reason is direct sex discrimination. There is no need for you to draw a comparison with a male employee in such cases. If you can establish that your treatment amounted to direct discrimination because of unfavourable treatment on the ground of your pregnancy, no question of justification for this treatment can arise.

Indirect discrimination

Indirect discrimination is more difficult to recognise and takes place where:

- your employer imposes a provision, rule or practice with which you cannot comply and which is to your disadvantage; and

- the condition or requirement can be shown to have a disproportionate impact in excluding others of your sex, marital status, race, sexual orientation or religion or religious belief; and

- the provision cannot be justified.

There is no protection against indirect discrimination in relation to gender reassignment or disability.

Please note that there is no requirement for you to show that you cannot comply with the provision, rule or practice; you just need to show it is to your disadvantage.

For example, indirect sex discrimination would take place where an employer imposed a requirement for all employees to be subject to a five-feet maximum height requirement. A much larger proportion of women than men would be able to meet this requirement and the employer would have to justify the reason for imposing such a condition. If the reason was because the job was to crew a boat with very low ceilings, such a requirement would probably be justified. But, if the reason was because the employer only wished to provide one size of uniform, the employer would be indirectly discriminating against men.

Justification requires an objective balance between the discriminatory effect of the provision, rule or practice and the reasonable needs of the employer who is applying it. Justification is a matter of judgment for the employment tribunal, which means that one tribunal may reach one conclusion and another may reach a different conclusion.

Sex discrimination – age

Although there is currently no law against age discrimination, placing restrictions on age can amount to indirect sex discrimination. This was the case where an employer imposed a maximum age limit of 28 for a job; this was indirectly discriminatory because in practice it was harder for women to comply with it than men, since women in their late 20s are commonly fully occupied with bringing up children.

Harassment

Harassment occurs where on the grounds of sex, marital status, gender reassignment, race, disability, sexual orientation, religion or belief, an employer behaves in a way that has the purpose or effect of violating an individual's dignity or creating an interrogating, hostile, degrading, humiliating or offensive environment for the individual.

Note that although harassment on the ground of disability is not expressly stated under the current legislation to be unlawful, it would amount to direct discrimination (i.e. less favourable treatment).

Harassment has a relatively wide definition and it can include physical, verbal and non-verbal conduct. For example, it would include the following types of behaviour:

- unwanted touching;

- molesting;
- assaulting;
- jokes;
- innuendos;
- pestering;
- threats;
- remarks;
- undirected banter;
- exclusion of an employee;
- written remarks;
- offensive pictures.

It does not matter if the harasser did not have the motive or intention of harassing – if the conduct is unwanted and it violates your dignity or creates an interrogating, hostile, degrading, humiliating or offensive environment, it will be unlawful harassment.

If you think you have been harassed, the best way of resolving the matter is to raise it with your employer as soon as possible, either informally or under its

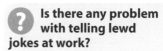

Is there any problem with telling lewd jokes at work?

Yes, if one of your colleagues finds them offensive, it could amount to harassment.

harassment or grievance policy (if it has one). It is very easy simply to think that any complaint you make will fall on deaf ears. But if you do not try, you do not know. Very often harassment in the form of jokes or innuendos can occur without the harasser realising that this is offensive to the victim. While this does not make the conduct acceptable, it is often easily resolved by letting the person know that such jokes or innuendos are offensive to you. Obviously, if the behaviour continues, or if you feel intimidated by the harasser, then raising it more formally with management or a member of personnel/human resources may be necessary. If your complaint is not dealt with, or if it is not dealt with to your satisfaction, you should seek advice either from the Equal Opportunities Commission, the Commission for

Racial Equality or the Disability Rights Commission (see
'Useful contacts' section) or a solicitor/legal advice centre as
to how to pursue your complaint in an employment tribunal.

Victimisation

Discrimination by victimisation exists if you have been treated
less favourably than others because you have brought, or
threatened to bring, proceedings, given evidence or
information, or taken any action or made any allegation against
your employer concerning the anti-discrimination laws.

Exceptions to discrimination protection

The law recognises that there are some circumstances where
there may be a good reason to give favourable treatment to a
particular sex/race, etc. In particular:

- **Positive discrimination.** If an employer identifies that
  one sex/race/sexual orientation/religion or belief, etc. is
  not properly represented within certain work areas, it
  may try to encourage individuals of that particular group
  to apply, by providing training or through an advertising
  campaign. Before doing this, the employer must be able
  to show that in the previous 12 months there have been
  either no individuals of that particular group or only
  a small proportion of them, carrying out the work
  in question. If not, the positive action will be
  discriminatory.

- Specific allowance is given that exempts Sikh men
  from the requirement to wear safety helmets while on
  construction sites.

- **Genuine occupational qualifications.** For some jobs,
  being of a certain sex/race/sexual orientation/religion or
  belief is a requirement. But attitudes and cultures are
  changing and an exception that was once acceptable may
  no longer be so. The applicability of the genuine
  occupational qualification exception is fairly limited.

- **National security.** Any action taken 'for the purpose of safeguarding national security' is not unlawful if it is justified for that purpose.

- **Benefits dependent on marital status.** It is not discriminatory for an employer to provide additional benefits that are dependent upon employees being married. Take, for example, an employer introducing a private medical insurance scheme to all employees, where the benefits extend to the spouses of employees who are married. This is not discriminatory. On the other hand, if the employer provides private health insurance cover to all employees and opposite-sex partners (whether married or unmarried), but not to same-sex partners, this would be discriminatory.

Employer responsibility for discrimination

Action for discrimination can be taken in the employment tribunal against both the individual discriminator and the employer. The employer is liable for anything done by its employees in the course of their employment, whether or not it was done with the employer's knowledge or approval.

However, your employer would not be liable if it could show that positive steps had been taken to address the possibility of discrimination occurring in the workplace. For example, your employer should have introduced and adhered to an equal opportunities policy which incorporates a harassment policy. All employees should have been made aware of such policies and been given training in their obligations not to discriminate, with any disciplinary action taken as necessary.

No 'contracting-out'

Your employer is not allowed to exclude or limit ('contract out' from) any provision of the discrimination laws in a contract of employment. If it does, it would have no effect, leaving you at liberty to bring a complaint against your employer in an employment tribunal. The exception to this would be if you and your employer entered into a binding compromise agreement on the termination of employment (see chapter 5).

Discrimination after employment has ended

When employment relationships have come to an end, the individual is still protected provided the discrimination arises out of, and is closely connected to, the employment relationship; the most obvious example would be where a former employer gives a discriminatory job reference.

Specific points relevant to particular forms of discrimination

Race discrimination

? Is racial discrimination just about someone's colour?

No, 'race' can also mean ethnic origin or nationality.

If a decision is based on your colour, race, nationality or national origins, or ethnic origins it is a decision based on racial grounds and could be discriminatory.

A group of people has an ethnic origin if it has the characteristics of:

*   a long shared history; and

*   a cultural tradition.

Additional relevant characteristics are:

*   a common geographical origin or descent from a small number of common ancestors;

*   a common language not necessarily peculiar to the group;

*   a common literature peculiar to the group;

*   a common religion different from that of the neighbouring or surrounding community;

- being a minority or being in an oppressed group in a large community.

Sikhs are an ethnic group, as are Jews and Gypsies, but at present Rastafarians have been judged not to fall within what can be considered an ethnic group.

In a sex discrimination claim, a comparison is made between a female employee and a male employee in equivalent circumstances in order to decide whether the treatment of one is less favourable. In a race discrimination claim, the comparison must be between the person of the racial or ethnic group and a job applicant or employee who is not of that ethnic or racial group, but whose circumstances are the same, similar or not significantly different.

If you want to complain of race discrimination and bring an action against your employer and/or the alleged discriminator, your burden of proving discrimination is slightly different from that of other forms of discrimination. First, you must establish the case and then your employer has to justify the alleged discriminatory act. If no explanation is forthcoming or an unsatisfactory explanation is provided, then the employment tribunal is entitled to conclude that discrimination did, in fact, take place.

Disability discrimination

It is unlawful for an employer to discriminate unjustifiably against a disabled person on the ground of disability. This law applies in a similar way to the current sex and race legislation at all stages in the recruitment process.

What kind of disability is protected by the anti-discrimination laws on disability? A disability is defined in this context as a physical or mental impairment which has a substantial and long-term adverse effect on a person's ability to carry out normal day-to-day activities.

Such a broad definition includes learning disabilities, mental illnesses (if recognised by a respected body of medical opinion), impairments that come and go if the actual effect is likely to recur (e.g. rheumatoid arthritis) and severe disfigurements. People with progressive conditions are covered from the moment the condition leads to impairment of their ability to carry out day-to-day activities. To be long-term, the condition must not be of a temporary nature and must have lasted 12 months or more or be likely to last 12 months or more. The definition specifically excludes some impairments, such as alcohol or drug addiction, hay fever and self-disfigurement (e.g. tattoos).

> **? Do the disability discrimination laws apply in our small office of six people?**
>
> *Yes, from October 2004 they have applied to all employers.*

Stress, which affects so many people nowadays in many different ways, will not, on its own, amount to a disability. However, if the stress is or becomes sufficiently serious to be a clinically recognised stress-related illness, this may amount to a disability within the anti-discrimination laws.

If you think that you may have a disability in this context, the best guidance you can follow is in a document issued by the Government entitled 'Guidance on Matters to be Taken into Account in Determining Questions Relating to the Definition of Disability'. A copy can be obtained by calling 0845 762 2633. The Disability Rights Commission may also be able to assist you (see 'Useful contacts' section).

Direct discrimination (less favourable treatment) of a disabled person will be allowable if the reason for it is both 'material' to the circumstances of the case and 'substantial'. This means that the reason has to relate to the individual circumstances in question and must not be trivial or minor.

Reasonable adjustments

Your employer has additional duties to make reasonable adjustments in relation to your disability. If any physical feature of your employer's premises or other arrangements cause a substantial disadvantage to you as a disabled person, your employer must make reasonable adjustments to prevent them.

Adjustments may include altering premises, reallocating duties, transferring staff to fill an existing vacancy, altering working hours, assigning someone to a different place of work, allowing absences from the office, training, acquiring or modifying equipment, modifying instructions or manuals, modifying procedures for testing or assessment and providing a reader or supervision. Whether it is reasonable for your employer to have to make a particular adjustment will depend upon a number of (often hard to judge) factors, including:

- how effective it would be in preventing the disadvantage;

- how practical it is;

- the financial and other costs involved and the disruption likely to be caused;

- the extent of the financial resources of your employer;

- the availability of assistance to make the adjustment.

Sexual orientation

You are protected from discrimination on the ground of your sexual orientation whether you are homosexual, heterosexual or bisexual. You are not protected against discrimination relating to particular sexual practices or fetishes.

Religion or belief

It is clear that people who belong to established religious traditions, such as Muslims, Jews and Catholics will be protected by this law. However, it is not clear whether non-conventional faiths or beliefs are covered, such as humanists, atheists or Rastafarians. The following factors should be considered when deciding on what is a religion or belief:

- Is there collective worship?

- Is there a clear belief system?

• Is it a profound belief affecting the way of life or the view of the world?

Political opinion or belief is not included within the definition.

Equal pay

If you consider you have received unequal treatment on the ground of your sex in the terms of your contract of employment, your claim is not for sex discrimination, but for equal pay. This typically occurs in matters such as salary, bonus payments and benefits.

> **Point of Law**
>
> *Equal Pay Act 1970*

The law on equal pay protects men as well as women and it benefits employees under a contract of employment as well as self-employed people under a contract for services. It does not apply to individuals who work wholly or mainly outside Great Britain, nor does it apply to members of the armed forces. You can claim equality if you can establish one of the following:

• that you are carrying out work which is the same or broadly similar to work being carried out by someone of the opposite sex in the same employment; or

• that you are carrying out work which has been rated as equal, through a job evaluation study, to work being carried out by someone of the opposite sex in the same employment; or

• that you are carrying out work which is of equal value to the work of someone of the opposite sex in the same employment.

Comparison

The comparison must be with a person of the opposite sex who exists (or has existed) who is doing similar work, work graded as equal or work of equal value and who is employed by the same employer (or an associated employer) either at the same establishment or at an establishment within Great Britain where, in general, common terms and conditions are observed.

> **? I am a woman who is paid less than a male colleague and yet we perform the same job. Is it fair?**
>
> *No, but it may be fair if he has been in the job longer than you.*

Defence

Your employer can successfully defend an equal pay claim if it can:

- prove that the work is not like or similar, not rated as equal or not of equal value; or

- prove that the difference between your contract and the comparison contract is genuinely due to a material factor which is not the difference in sex.

Equality clause

If you can establish that one of the above three justifications for equality applies and your contract contains terms less beneficial than those enjoyed by the comparison person of the opposite sex, or which omits a beneficial term enjoyed by that person, you can apply to an employment tribunal to have an equality clause implied into your contract. Such a clause modifies your contract so that it is equivalent to the comparison person's contract.

Other remedies

In addition to an equality clause in the contract, you may be awarded compensation for loss suffered in the past as a result of lack of equality.

What should you do if you are the victim of discrimination?

If, having considered the different forms of discrimination discussed in this chapter, you consider you may have been discriminated against, the first step you need to take is to check whether your employer has any internal policies that set out a procedure for you to raise a complaint of discrimination. If it does, then you must raise your concerns in line with this procedure. If there is no such policy, then you should simply raise the matter either with your line manager, or if it is the line manager whom you wish to complain about, then another, more senior, member of management or someone in the personnel/human resources team. Only if you have exhausted all avenues for seeking to resolve your concerns internally should you consider taking legal action in an employment tribunal. However, there is no need for you to leave your employment before taking legal action for discrimination against your employer. There are various bodies who may be able to assist you in taking legal action against your employer and they are detailed in the 'Useful contacts' section.

Your claim for discrimination must be made in an employment tribunal within three months of the act of discrimination. It may be difficult to identify the act of discrimination so you should be careful about ensuring the claim is brought within the time limit. Some discrimination continues over a period of time (e.g. if you are being subjected to continuing harassment), often up to the date of leaving employment. Provided you can show continuing discrimination then the three months will run from the last act of discrimination.

However, if it is a single act of discrimination such as a failed promotion, even if it has continuing effects (such as continuing employment at a lower grade and salary), the claim must be made within three months from the decision not to promote. It may be that you have raised an internal gricvance against the failed promotion. The failure of the grievance procedure itself may be alleged to be an act of discrimination, in which case the three months will run from the decision of the grievance procedure.

The employment tribunal may allow a claim that is brought outside the three-month time limit if it is just and fair to do so. It will consider factors such as the reason for the delay, the degree of lateness, the strength of the case, whether there is any harm done by the late filing of the claim, and the chances of there still being a fair hearing of the matter. Generally, an employment tribunal should not lightly deprive you of your right to bring a claim, so if the above factors are persuasive, it would be worth trying to obtain agreement of the tribunal to allow the claim out of time.

> **? Is there a time limit for making a discrimination claim in an employment tribunal?**
>
> *Yes, three months from the last incident.*

Questionnaires

If you think you have been discriminated against, before you begin proceedings you may wish to make use of the questionnaire procedure which is specific to discrimination cases to obtain information from your employer to help you decide whether you do have a claim. You can also use this procedure after proceedings have begun provided the questionnaire is served on your employer within 21 days of filing your claim with the employment tribunal.

The questionnaire procedure allows you to interrogate your employer or former employer about reasons for taking any relevant action or on any other matter that is or may be relevant. There are standard questionnaire forms that you can obtain from a legal adviser or from the Commission for Racial Equality. The questionnaire procedure can be an invaluable tool in obtaining relevant information from your employer and the questions and replies may be used as evidence in tribunal proceedings. If your employer fails, without reasonable excuse, to respond to the questionnaire or provides an evasive response, the employment tribunal may draw any inference from that fact, including an inference that your employer has committed an unlawful act of discrimination.

CHAPTER 5

The end of the relationship

Termination by your employer

If you lose your job, the two main things you need to consider
are whether your employer has terminated your employment
in accordance with your contract and whether your dismissal
is fair or unfair (under the law of unfair dismissal, discussed
in this chapter). You may also need to consider whether
dismissal has been discriminatory (see chapter 4).

Contract

The proper notice that your employer must give should be
specified in your contract of employment. If a notice period has
not been expressly agreed, your employment may be
terminated upon 'reasonable' notice. What is reasonable
depends on factors such as your seniority, age, length of service,
remuneration and what is usual in your profession or industry.

Whatever the contractual
provisions for termination
of the contract, the notice
actually given must not be
less than the statutory
minimum period of notice
(see chapter 1). If proper

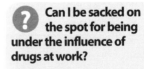

**Can I be sacked on
the spot for being
under the influence of
drugs at work?**

*No, your employer must follow
a disciplinary procedure
before taking action.*

notice is given, you will have no claim for compensation. However, you may still have a valid claim for unfair dismissal even if proper notice is given.

Whether you or your employer are terminating your employment, it is common for the employer to want you to cease working immediately. This is often because of the risk that you may not continue to work effectively and that you may be disruptive in the workplace. In these circumstances, it is usual for your employer to pay you a sum in lieu of notice or as compensation for failure to give notice.

Sometimes the contract will expressly provide that it may be terminated on payment of a sum in lieu of notice. In these circumstances when the payment is made, tax and National Insurance deductions should be made in the usual way.

If there is nothing in the contract relating to making payments in lieu, the payment may be paid tax-free up to a limit of £30,000 and without deduction of National Insurance contributions. It is not always entirely clear whether the payment is tax-free, so it is worth seeking advice on this point.

Point of Law
Income Tax (Earnings and Pensions) Act 2003

If a payment in lieu of notice is made, it is not only your salary, but also all benefits, such as a company car, that must be included in the calculation. The exception to this would be if your contract stated that pay in lieu of notice does not include benefits.

Dismissal without notice and without pay in lieu of notice entitles you to claim damages for your notice pay and benefits; this claim is known as wrongful dismissal. The exception is if you are guilty of gross misconduct, in which case your employer would be justified in dismissing you with immediate effect. What constitutes gross misconduct does depend upon the work environment. Examples of gross misconduct are theft, damage to the employer's property, incapacity for work due to being under the influence of alcohol or illegal drugs, physical assault and gross insubordination, or misuse of email and the Internet.

Unfair dismissal

If you are dismissed without a fair reason, or without your employer following a fair procedure, this is likely to be unfair. Your dismissal will be for a potentially fair reason if it is:

- connected to your capability or qualifications for performing your job; this covers both performance-related dismissals and sickness absence dismissals; or

- connected to your conduct;

- redundancy;

- because you could not continue to work in the position which you held without breaking the law (e.g. a lorry driver losing a driving licence); or

- connected with some other substantial reason of a kind sufficient to justify your dismissal.

If the reason or principal reason for dismissal is one of the above, the next step is to consider whether under the circumstances dismissal was actually fair or unfair. This depends on all the circumstances surrounding the dismissal including the size and administrative resources of your employer. One of the decisive factors at this stage is whether or not your employer followed a fair procedure.

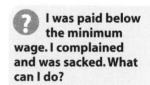

I was paid below the minimum wage. I complained and was sacked. What can I do?

Dismissal was automatically unfair; consider claiming in the employment tribunal.

There are some circumstances when dismissal is deemed to be automatically unfair. This is the case if dismissal is for one of the following reasons:

- your membership or non-membership of an independent trade union or because you have taken part in activities of an independent trade union;

- a maternity-related reason;

- an adoption-related reason;

- a paternity-related reason;

- a health and safety reason;

- because you asserted your statutory rights;

- because you performed duties as an employee representative (or were a candidate to be an employee representative);

- because you performed duties as a pension scheme trustee;

- because of the transfer of an undertaking, i.e. where the ownership of the employer is transferred from one person/entity to another;

- a spent conviction or failure to disclose a spent conviction;

- selection for redundancy for any of the above reasons;

- taking parental leave or taking time off for dependants;

- making a protected disclosure (i.e. whistleblowing);

- a National Minimum Wage reason;

- enforcing a right to Working Family Tax Credit; or

- taking part in protected industrial action.

In addition, since October 2004 failure by an employer to comply with statutory dispute resolution procedures will render a dismissal automatically unfair.

Qualifying conditions

To bring a claim for unfair dismissal, you must have been employed under a contract for a minimum continuous period of one year. In addition, you must not be over normal retirement age or, if there is no retirement age, 65.

The time limit for bringing a claim for unfair dismissal is three months from the termination of the contract. An employment tribunal will extend the time limit in certain circumstances (e.g. severe illness, meaning you cannot submit the claim in time) and it is therefore recommended that you do submit your claim well within the three-month time limit.

No qualifying period of service is required if the dismissal is due to:

- membership or non-membership of an independent trade union or taking part in activities of an independent trade union;

- a maternity-related reason;

- an adoption-related reason;

- a paternity-related reason;

- a health and safety reason;

- asserting statutory rights;

- the performance of duties as employee representative (or being a candidate due to become an employee representative);

- the performance of duties as a pension scheme trustee;

- refusing to work on a Sunday as a shop or betting shop worker;

- a reason connected with the Working Time Regulations;

- a reason related to making protected disclosure (i.e. 'whistleblowing');

- a reason related to securing the benefit of the National Minimum Wage;

- enforcing a right to Working Family Tax Credits; or

- taking part in protected industrial action.

If you are dismissed on medical grounds specified in any health and safety at work law, regulation or code of practice, you can make a claim for unfair dismissal, provided you have one month's continuous employment.

Remedies

You may seek reinstatement (for you to return to your original job), re-engagement (for you to be placed in a job comparable to that from which you were dismissed or other suitable employment) or compensation (up to a statutory maximum limit). Orders for reinstatement or re-engagement are rare, but if you want to be considered for these, then, if you are successful in your claim, an employment tribunal must consider whether one would be appropriate.

Compensation is the most common remedy and usually comprises a basic award and a compensatory award. In addition, there are further awards made in certain circumstances, such as an 'additional award', if your employer fails to comply with an order for reinstatement or re-engagement, and a 'special award' if your employer fails to comply with an order for reinstatement or re-engagement where dismissal was on the grounds of trade union membership/activities or health and safety duties.

(i) Basic award

The basic award is calculated by considering your age, length of continuous service and gross average weekly wage. Each complete year of service up to a maximum of 20 counts for payment on the following scale (with a current maximum of £280 for a week's pay):

- up to 22 years of age – ½ week's pay;

- between 22 and up to 41 years of age – 1 week's pay;

- between 41 and up to 65 years of age – 1½ weeks' pay.

Where employees are dismissed after their 64th birthday, the basic award is reduced by one-twelfth for every month after that.

The current maximum basic award is £8,400 (i.e. 1½ × 20 × 280).

An employment tribunal will reduce the basic award if it considers it to be just and reasonable to do so.

(ii) Compensatory award

The compensatory award is calculated on the net value of wages, other benefits and expenses reasonably incurred by you as a result of the dismissal.

Factors an employment tribunal will then take into account to reduce the award are:

- contributory fault;
- whether dismissal would have resulted even if your employer had acted reasonably;
- your duty to minimise your loss by attempting to seek other employment;
- payments made by your employer;
- what is just and reasonable, including whether there has been an injury to your feelings brought about by the manner of your dismissal.

Once the assessment of the compensatory award has been made as described above, the statutory limit, currently £56,800, will be applied. This statutory limit does not apply where the dismissal is as a result of making a protected disclosure (i.e. 'whistleblowing').

For dismissals that occur after 1 October 2004 the compensatory award may be increased or decreased by between 10 and 50 per cent for failure to comply with the statutory dispute resolution procedures depending on which

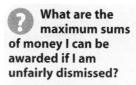

What are the maximum sums of money I can be awarded if I am unfairly dismissed?

A basic award of up to £8,100 plus a compensatory award of up to £56,800, depending on the circumstances.

party is at fault (subject to the statutory cap of £56,800).

Damages for injury to feelings (e.g. humiliation, distress, damage to reputation) brought about by the manner of dismissal are only likely to be awarded in limited circumstances, and may be dependent on you producing medical evidence of the effect of the way you were dismissed (not just the fact it happened). If an award is appropriate, the level is likely to be in line with the following bands: £500 to £5,000 for less serious cases; £5,000 to £15,000 in serious cases; and £15,000 to £25,000 in the most serious cases. However, note that this element is not in addition to the statutory limit of £56,800.

Redundancy

Point of Law
Employment Rights Act 1996

As indicated above, redundancy is a potentially fair reason for dismissal. However, it will only be fair if a genuine redundancy situation exists and if your employer has carried out a fair procedure in selecting you for redundancy which must include consultation with you about the redundancy.

A genuine redundancy situation exists where your dismissal was attributable wholly or mainly to the fact that:

- your employer has ceased, or intends to cease, carrying on the business for which you were employed or has ceased, or intends to cease, carrying it on at a place where you were employed (i.e. relocation); or

- the business's need for work for which you were taken on has, or is expected to, cease or diminish (i.e. a reduction in the number of employees is required).

Once your employer has told you that you are at risk of redundancy, provided you have two years' service, you can take reasonable paid time off to look for a new job or to arrange training for a new job.

Even if your dismissal for redundancy is fair, you may still be entitled to a Statutory Redundancy Payment.

Statutory Redundancy Payment

You will be entitled to a Statutory Redundancy Payment if you have at least two years' service after reaching the age of 18. The entitlement is calculated in the same way as the basic award for unfair dismissal claims (see above) except employment prior to reaching 18 is not counted and if you are made redundant after your 64th birthday, the payment is reduced by one-twelfth for every month after that.

You may raise a complaint with an employment tribunal within six months of termination if you have not received the correct redundancy payment. The time limit may be extended for a further six months if approved by the employment tribunal.

> **? I have been made redundant. What compensation is there?**
>
> *If you have two years' service, you are entitled to Statutory Redundancy Payment from your employer as a minimum.*

You are not entitled to Statutory Redundancy Payment if, before the existing job ends, your employer offers you (verbally or in writing) employment on the same terms or suitable alternative work, beginning within four weeks of the ending of the original employment. If you unreasonably refuse such an offer, or during a trial period for the new job unreasonably terminate such employment, you lose the right to Statutory Redundancy Payment.

If you leave your job before dismissal takes effect and your employer objects in writing, the employment tribunal may determine the extent of your entitlement.

Termination by you

Resignation

If you wish to resign, this should be with notice. The period of notice that you must give is subject to a statutory minimum of one week, although your contractual notice period will in many cases be longer, so you should check your contract.

You are entitled to continue to receive all salary and benefits for the notice period provided you are ready and willing to work for that period. However, you and your employer may agree that you should stop working before the end of the full notice period.

Sometimes resignations occur as a result of an argument or a falling out with your boss or line manager. If you do resign in the heat of the moment and subsequently regret it, you should tell your employer you did not mean to resign. If your employer holds you to the resignation and your job is terminated, your employment may then be deemed to be terminated by dismissal by your employer rather than by your resignation and you may have a right to bring a claim of unfair dismissal.

> **?** **I formally resigned and now regret my decision, do I have to go?**
>
> *That depends on whether your employer is willing to take you back; it is not obliged to.*

Subject to resignations in the heat of the moment, however, once your employer has accepted your resignation you may not withdraw the resignation without your employer's consent.

If you resign without giving notice, you will be in breach of contract, unless it is in response to a fundamental breach of contract by your employer (i.e. constructive dismissal). If you do resign without giving notice, your employer can contractually require you to serve out the period of notice that you should have given, but in practice this would be very difficult to enforce because a court would never compel you to work. However, your employer would not have to pay you for any time after the date of resignation. In theory, your employer could also sue you for damages for losses incurred as a result of your breach of contract by you not working your notice. But in practice it is often impossible to prove what losses have been incurred (except in the case of very senior executives) and such claims are very rarely brought.

Sometimes your employer may want you to serve out the correct period of notice to prevent you from immediately joining a competitor. Alternatively, there may be a clause in your contract restraining you (after leaving your job) from working for a competitor. These clauses are only enforceable if they are reasonably required for the protection of your employer's legitimate business interests.

Alternatively, or in addition, your employer may have included what is known as a 'garden leave' clause in your contract requiring you to remain at home during your notice. The aim is to prevent you from leaving to work for a competitor while not having you around at work where you may obtain confidential information. If you have restrictive clauses or garden leave clauses in your contract of employment and want to know how this affects what you can and cannot do after leaving your employment, you should consult a solicitor.

Constructive dismissal

Constructive dismissal is a term that is used regularly in today's workplace, but its meaning is often misunderstood. You may have a valid claim for constructive unfair and wrongful dismissal if your employer's conduct towards

 What exactly is constructive dismissal?

When you resign because your employer's conduct fundamentally breaches your contract.

you is such that it is in fundamental breach of your contract of employment. Your employer's conduct would need to be more than simply unreasonable and would have to include things such as reducing your pay without your consent, bullying or harassment or failing to deal with a harassment complaint, or reducing your status without your consent. In order to bring a claim, you would have to resign first (with or without notice).

Resigned or constructively dismissed?

If you do complain of unfair constructive dismissal, your employer may argue that you resigned and that dismissal did not occur. You would have to prove that your employer's conduct clearly breached and repudiated the contract entitling you to leave without notice and you considered that the contract was at an end because of your employer's conduct.

Constructive dismissal often occurs as a result of a breach of the implied terms of trust and confidence (i.e. a breakdown in the employment relationship). This can be caused by a single action by your employer (such as verbal abuse) or by a series of less serious actions which together amount to a breach of the term.

If your employer makes a statement of clear intention to breach an essential term of the contract, you can leave and claim constructive dismissal based on an anticipatory breach of the contract.

If you consider you have been constructively dismissed, you should seek advice before taking the decision to resign and, in any event, you must raise an internal grievance with your employer to comply with the statutory dispute resolution procedure and to avoid being barred from bringing a claim in the employment tribunal. However, it is important that you act quickly. If you do not leave soon after the incident or incidents complained of, your employer can argue that you accepted the alleged breach and that therefore no constructive dismissal occurred.

Termination by mutual agreement

You and your employer may mutually agree to end your employment. If you are forced to agree to the termination with the threat of dismissal, you may still have a claim for unfair dismissal. Financial inducements to agree to terminate your employment are acceptable.

If you and your employer mutually agree to end the contract, there is no need for your employer to give notice of termination. You will have no entitlement to pay in lieu of notice or redundancy pay. However, it is fairly usual for the employer to make a payment described as an 'ex gratia payment' to avoid any implication of unfair dismissal.

Settlements

Where there is a dispute, the parties will often prefer to settle the matter rather than proceed to a hearing. A binding settlement can be reached in one of the following ways:

Advisory, Conciliation and Arbitration Service conciliation

If, once you have filed a claim in the employment tribunal, you would like to explore the possibility of settling your claim, you should contact the ACAS conciliation officer who will have been allocated to your case. You should receive a letter of introduction from this conciliation officer; if you do not hear from anyone, simply contact ACAS, who will locate the officer for you.

Compromise agreements

Point of Law
Section 203 Employment Rights Act 1996

Another way to settle a dispute is for you and your employer to make a compromise agreement. For a compromise agreement to be effective, it must be in writing and must fulfil the following conditions:

- It must relate to the particular complaint.

- You must have received independent legal advice from a qualified lawyer, an officer of an independent trade union or a worker at an advice centre as to the terms and effect of the proposed agreement, and in particular its effects on your ability to pursue the appropriate rights before an employment tribunal. The adviser who gives the advice must have an insurance policy covering the risk of a claim by you for an alleged loss arising out of the advice.

? Is the employment tribunal the only way to settle a dispute?

No, you can try conciliation through ACAS or formally agree to compromise.

- The agreement must identify the adviser.

- The agreement must declare that the above conditions are satisfied.

Useful contacts

Advisory, Conciliation and Arbitration Service (ACAS)
Head Office
Brandon House
180 Borough High Street
London SE1 1LW
Helpline: 0845 747 4747
Website: www.acas.org.uk

Advisory Conciliation and Arbitration Service (ACAS) – Scottish Division
151 West George Street
Glasgow G2 7JJ
Tel: 0141 248 1400

Commission for Racial Equality (CRE)
Head Office
St Dunstan's House
201–211 Borough High Street
London SE1 1GZ
Tel: 020 7939 0000
Website: www.cre.gov.uk

Criminal Records Bureau
PO Box 110
Liverpool L69 3EF
Tel: 0870 909 0811
Website: www.crb.gov.uk

Department of Trade and Industry (DTI)
DTI Enquiry Unit
1 Victoria Street
London SW1H 0ET

Tel: 020 7215 5000
Email: dti.enquiries@dti.gsi.gov.uk
Website: www.dti.gov.uk

Department for Work and Pensions (DWP)
Correspondence Unit, Room 540, The Adelphi
1–11 John Adam Street
London WC2N 6HT
Tel: 020 7712 2171(*general enquiries*)
Website: www.dfwp.gov.uk

Disability Rights Commission
FREEPOST MID02164
Stratford upon Avon CV37 9BR
Tel: 0845 762 2633
Textphone: 0845 762 2644
Website: www.drc-gb.org

Employment Appeal Tribunal
Audit House
58 Victoria Embankment
London EC4Y 0DS
Tel: 020 7273 1040
Website: www.employmentappeals.gov.uk

Employment Appeal Tribunal – Scottish Division
52 Melville Street
Edinburgh EH3 7HS
Tel: 0131 225 3963

Employment Tribunal Central Enquiries
100 Southgate Street
Bury St Edmunds IP33 2AQ
Tel: 0845 795 9775
Website: www.employmenttribunals.gov.uk

Equal Opportunities Commission
Arndale House
Arndale Centre
Manchester M4 3EQ
Tel: 0845 601 5901
Website: www.eoc.org.uk

European Commission
8 Storey's Gate
London SW1P 3AT
Tel: 020 7973 1992
Website: www.cec.org.uk

European Court of Justice
Cour de justice des Communautés européennes
L-2925 Luxembourg
Tel: 00 352 430 31
Website: www.curia.eu.int

Health and Safety Executive Books
PO Box 1999
Sudbury
Suffolk CO10 2WA
Tel: 01787 881 165
Website: www.hsebooks.co.uk

Health and Safety Executive's Infoline
Caerphilly Business Park
Caerphilly CF83 3GG
Helpline: 0870 154 5500
Email: hseinformationservices@natbrit.com
Website: www.hse.gov.uk

Home Office
Work Permits (UK)
PO Box 3468
Sheffield
Tel: 0114 259 4074
Email: wpcustomers@ind.homeoffice.gsi.gov.uk
Website: www.workingintheuk.gov.uk

Jobcentre Plus Secretariat
Correspondence Manager
Ground Floor, Steel City House
West Street
Sheffield S1 2GQ
Tel: 0845 601 2001 (*employers*)
     0845 606 0234 (*job seekers*)
Website: www.jobcentreplus.gov.uk

Office of the Informatiom Commissioner
Data Protection Commissioner
Wycliffe House, Water Lane
Wilmslow SK9 5AF
Tel: 01625 545 700
Website: www.informationcommissioner.gov.uk

Race Relations Employment Advisory Service
4th Floor, 2 Duchess Place
Hagley Road
Birmingham B16 8NS
Tel: 0121 452 5447/8/9

Index